THIS BOOK BELONGS
TO

MARK RICHARD WORRALL

1 NEW STATION ROAD

SWINTON

SOUTH YORKSHIRE

S64 8AH

CW00550700

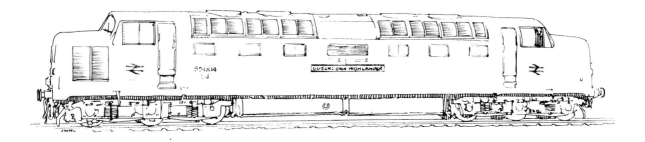

PROFILE
OF THE
DELTICS

◁ On 16th October, 1976 No 55 003 *Meld* speeds through
Peterborough heading the down "Aberdonian", the 12.10
Kings Cross—Edinburgh and Aberdeen. On the left
No 47 078 *Sir Daniel Gooch* awaits its next duty.　　*J S Whiteley*

On 7th March, 1976 No 55 017 *The Durham Light Infantry*
eases out of Newcastle over the River Tyne on the King
Edward Bridge heading the Sunday 11.40 Edinburgh—Kings
Cross.

P J Robinson

PROFILE OF THE DELTICS

BY
J.S. WHITELEY
&
G.W. MORRISON

Oxford Publishing Co.

Above   In its eye-catching light blue, grey and cream livery, the prototype Deltic is descending from Stoke Summit to Grantham whilst heading a down semi-fast on 30th May, 1959. *T Boustead.*

Right and Below   After successful trials with the prototype, twenty-two production models appeared from early 1961 and until 1979 have successfully handled the accelerated Inter-City services on the East Coast main line. By 1979 they were being replaced by HST units on the principal services, but in the twilight of their life they were diagrammed to haul the down "Hull Executive" from Kings Cross on an extremely fast timing of 2 hours 50 minutes to Hull, averaging almost 92 mph from Kings Cross to its first stop at Retford. No 55 003 *Meld* is seen on 15th May, 1979 approaching Doncaster, and leaving after its brief stop.

G W Morrison

ACKNOWLEDGEMENT

The preparation of our second Deltic album has been no less enjoyable than the first, and our thanks are offered to fellow photographers who have contributed pictures, John Holroyd for his help with the art work, Margaret Morley for typing the manuscript and to our publishers for the freedom given to us during its preparation.

Typesetting and Art Production by Katerprint Co Ltd, Cowley Oxford

Printed by
Blackwell's in the City of Oxford

Published by Oxford Publishing Co.
8 The Roundway
Headington
Oxford

SBN 86093 102 1

A wintry scene on 18th March, 1979 as No 55 013 *The Black Watch* passes through Marsh Lane cutting, Leeds, heading the Sunday 13.50 Leeds—Kings Cross. It was being diverted via Selby because of engineering work between Wakefield and Doncaster.

J S Whiteley

Introduction *by Allan C. Baker*

If, ten years ago, anybody had suggested to me that diesel locomotives would attract the attention they are then I, together with many others, would have gasped in disbelief; but so it is. The "Warships", "Hymeks" and the "Westerns" all attracted an enormous following of enthusiasts old and new during their twilight years; now dawns the final fling of the "Deltics".

The demise of this particular class seems to be attracting more interest than ever, but, perhaps because the class has only ever numbered twenty two, the "Deltics" have always tended to be considered as something a little special. Like the hydraulic classes before them, one hears of preservation schemes and one hopes that one, at least, is successful; however, I fear the magnitude of the task if those intrepid fellows intend to keep one running!

Until comparatively recently the "Deltics" were just another type of diesel locomotive to me, until that is, I found myself at Finsbury Park Depot, the East Coast main line London diesel shed. Coming as I did from the London Midland Region there were many things new to me, but perhaps the "Deltic" was one of the most outstanding. I was soon struck by the awe with which they were held, not only by the maintenance and footplate staff, but by almost everybody. At Finsbury Park we had the racehorses, named in splendid LNER tradition and favourites all, not that we ever referred to them by their names or even proper numbers, just No 3 or No 7.

Much has been and no doubt will be written about these locomotives, and it cannot be doubted that the concept of putting engines designed for marine applications, moreover extremely arduous and specialist ones, into a locomotive proved a winner, albeit a relatively expensive one. The planners got what they wanted, 3,300 installed horsepower for an overall locomotive weight of no more than 100 tons, the most powerful single unit diesel locomotive in the world in 1960, a record still held for this country no less than twenty years on. What finer accolade could the class claim?

Unfortunately, although not perhaps surprisingly, this two-stroke, opposed piston, three crankshaft engine brought with it many inherent problems, and an engine completely unlike anything else in use then, or since, on British Railways and that, in itself, has caused many of the problems in their maintenance and repair ever since. However, in fairness, the class's low availability over the last few years has often been due to a spare part supply problem frequently outside the control of the railway. Nevertheless, over the years a considerable expertise has been built up amongst the depots to which the class has been allocated, not forgetting Doncaster Works, a most vital link in the chain.

There have always been considerably more engines than needed for the twenty two locomotives and these could be changed over at Doncaster Works in around two or three eight hour shifts. Thus, with the locomotives working the East Coast main line passenger service, it was an easy matter to get them into and out of the "Plant" for engine changes if defects arose which the depots could not handle, and little could be accomplished in the way of engine repairs without removing them from the locomotives. Similarly, by keeping a close watch on the condition of engines nearing their overhaul periods, with the use of experienced technical riding inspectors, engines could often be kept running well over the norm depending on the supply position of repaired units. Conversely, engines showing signs of defects could be taken out of service before these became serious. It all worked very nicely and kept the East Coast main line in the forefront of locomotive performance well into the days of its electrified West Coast sister, but there was a price to pay for this performance which was high in comparison with other diesel types, and it caused many to question their continued use.

On the depot the problems were many and varied, not least the extremely cramped conditions within the engine room with those two Napier "Deltic" engines, their associated generators and electrical control gear, and not least a Spanner Mk II train heating boiler in the middle. One of the most awkward jobs for the maintenance staff was fuel injector renewal, 18 per engine and a task despised by almost all, yet one requiring such expert care and attention and being ideal for Fitters but four feet tall! The use of two separate engines and their electrical systems in a diesel electric locomotive was not very popular in this country and here again problems were encountered with staff more accustomed to simpler single engine designs.

Because of the necessity of the diagrammed number being available each day to maintain the East Coast main line service to timetable, considerable priority was always given to the class; at Finsbury Park we tried to make a point of keeping time "stopped" to a minimum and only have one of our eight "stopped" at any one time. As the locomotives got older and more repairs arose, this sometimes became difficult. As a result of these efforts by all depots, and not forgetting Doncaster Works, the mileages accrued by the fleet over the years stand streets above any other diesel locomotive before or since.

When Gavin Morrison and John Whiteley first invited me to pen this short introduction, I accepted with open arms for it gives me, a locomotive man all my life, an opportunity to pay my tribute to a class of locomotive which has been so much a part of my daily life for the past five years or so. When the last "Deltic" makes its final journey I, together with very many others, will feel a similar nostalgic regret to one felt many years ago when the last Stanier Pacific arrived on Crewe North shed after its final journey. Had anybody suggested to me but a few years ago that one day I might mourn the end of a diesel class, I would have retaliated quite strongly, but such is the attraction of this famous class. Never do I hear the full throated roar of a "Deltic" engine without a feeling of admiration for a locomotive which in all circumstances seemed, and indeed was, fully master of its job.

I am sure that many of you will have seen Gavin and John's previous album, and what a splendid volume it is; here you have a second instalment, no less interesting than the first and carrying the "Deltic" story in pictures almost up to the present day. With the May 1979 timetable it was good to see the class regularly diagrammed to haul the country's fastest locomotive hauled train, the down "Hull Executive"— 17.05 ex Kings Cross. For our part at Finsbury Park it was good to give the racehorses a little individuality by restoring the white cab ends they had when they were new, and if this serves, as I think it does, to increase interest in our railway by enthusiast, general public and railwayman alike, then what better could a depot do?

It cannot be denied that the end is not far away, the locomotives have served us well and must, despite heavy repair costs, have paid for themselves time and time again. However, as more modern forms of traction come along, as must inevitably happen, the "Deltics", like the Stirling Singles, Ivatt Atlantics and Gresley Pacifics before them, must bow down to the never ending march of progress. I salute them in their passing.

London.
April 1980

55 001

Plate 1 Above   The Sunday 10.05 Bradford—Kings Cross is hurried through the outskirts of Leeds at Beeston on 26th June, 1977. No 55 001 was the first Deltic to be delivered, on 23rd February, 1961, and was one of eight named after famous racehorses, all of which are still allocated to Finsbury Park at the time of writing.   *G W Morrison*

Plate 2 Above   On 3rd September, 1977 No 55 002 leaves platform 9 at York on the Saturday 08.30 Newcastle—Kings Cross. This was one of the six Gateshead Deltics, none of which were especially renowned for their cleanliness.

G W Morrison

Plate 3 Below   It is seen in the lovely Scottish Border Country near Horn Burn on the Saturday 10.40 Edinburgh—Kings Cross on 6th August, 1977.

G W Morrison

55 003

Plate 4 Above   At rest between duties at Finsbury Park on
Saturday 30th July, 1977.   *G W Morrison*

Plate 5 Below   *Meld* was the first of the Finsbury Park
Deltics to receive white cab roofs, in April 1979, with
several more being similarly treated later in the Spring. It is
seen on 6th June, 1979 approaching the entrance to Stoke
Tunnel at High Dyke on the 12.15 York–Kings Cross. Note
also number at both ends.   *J S Whiteley*

Plate 6 Above No 55 004 *Queen's Own Highlander* was one of the six Deltics given Regimental names which had previously not been used on locomotives. It is seen bringing empty stock through Leeds station on 7th May, 1977 having arrived very late from Kings Cross earlier in the day.

J S Whiteley

Plate 7 Below This was one of eight Deltics allocated to Haymarket after delivery in 1961 and it is seen at rest in Kings Cross yard on 31st July, 1977.

G W Morrison

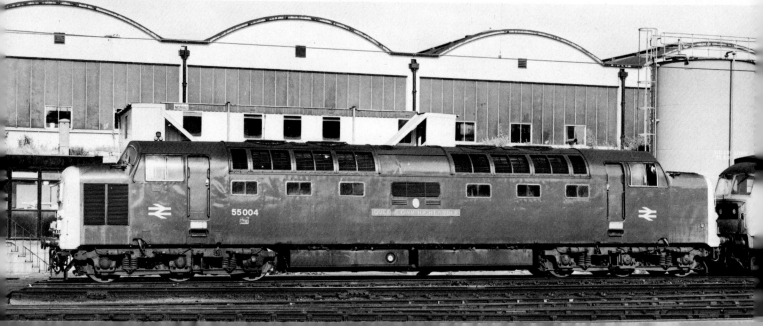

55 005

Plate 8 Above   When the Deltics were introduced they were painted in attractive two-tone green livery, as seen here, with the yellow warning panel on the nose added later. They were originally numbered D 9000—9021, and they were renumbered 55 001—55 022 late 1973/early 1974, No D 9000 becoming No 55 022. As No D 9005 it is passing Wortley South Junction on its climb out of Leeds heading the up "Queen of Scots Pullman" on 1st July, 1965.   *G W Morrison*

Plate 9 Below   As renumbered 55 005 it is emerging from Stoke Tunnel on 11th June, 1978 heading the 12.00 Kings Cross— Edinburgh.   *J S Whiteley*

Plate 10 Above   After arrival at platform 16 at York on the 18.05 slow from Kings Cross on 2nd October, 1979.
J S Whiteley

Plate 11 Below   No 55 006 draws to a halt at Selby on the 18.11 York—Kings Cross stopping train. 12th July, 1979.
G W Morrison

55 007

Plate 12 Above   Saturday 4th August, 1979 sees No 55 007 *Pinza* running round its train at Edinburgh after arrival on one of the shuttle trains from Dunbar during the closure of Penmanshiel Tunnel.

G W Morrison

Plate 13 Left On 2nd June, 1977 it is head ing the SX 16.52 Harrogate—Kings Cross near Bentley. By this date the route indi cator panel was not used by BR but it had not received the modifications as seen in the previous picture.

G W Morrison

Plate 14 Below The station clock shows 23.10 as No 55 008 stands at platform 9, York, on the murky evening of 2nd October 1979, whilst it is heading the 20.00 sleeper from Kings Cross to Aberdeen.

J S Whiteley

Plate 15 Right   The down "Talisman", the 16.00 Kings Cross—Edinburgh, approaches York on 26th May, 1977 behind No 55 009. In the background a class 37 approaches on an oil train.

J S Whiteley

Plate 16 Below   On 29th June, 1979 it is seen passing King Edward Bridge Junction, Gateshead, on the 20.30 passenger and postal from Newcastle to Kings Cross. It has left Newcastle via the High Level Bridge, and Gateshead MPD can be seen behind the rear of the train.

N Stead

Plate 17 Left The south end of Doncaster sees No 55 010 passing on the up "Leeds Executive" on its scheduled non-stop journey of 2 hours 30 minutes to Kings Cross.

J S Whiteley

Plate 18 Below The Sunday 10.00 Kings Cross—Aberdeen restarts from platform 9 at York on 5th March, 1978.

J S Whiteley

Plate 19 Right After its stop at Darlington, No 55 011 accelerates the 08.00 Edinburgh—Kings Cross on its journey south on 14th May, 1977. The non-stop through lines can be seen to the right hand side of the station.

G W Morrison

Plate 20 Below A telephoto lens exaggerates the curvature of Chaloners Whin Junction, York, as No 55 011 joins the lines from Sheffield and Leeds whilst heading the 14.00 Kings Cross—Aberdeen. 16th May, 1977.

J S Whiteley

Plate 21 Above The 18.58 Newcastle—Kings Cross glints in the evening sun at Low Fell on 21st April, 1979.

R Lumley

Plate 22 Below Heading the Sunday 10.00 Kings Cross—Edinburgh and Aberdeen, No 55 012 crosses from the slow to the fast lines at the top of Holloway Bank on 31st July, 1977.

G W Morrison

55 013

Plate 23 Above   On the wet morning of 28th April, 1977, the 11.55 to Kings Cross is accelerated up the gradient from Bradford Exchange, past St. Dunstans.

G W Morrison

Plate 24 Left Before the route indicator panel was filled in, No 55 014 is passing Laisterdyke on 26th May, 1977 with the 11.55 Bradford–Kings Cross.
J S Whiteley

Plate 25 Below It is approaching Newark on 12th May, 1979 heading the 14.45 Kings Cross–Leeds, just before the full introduction of HST units on West Riding services.
G W Morrison

55 015

Plate 26 Above   Passing through Doncaster on the down "Silver Jubilee" on 7th July, 1977.   *G W Morrison*

Plate 27 Below   It is travelling at about 100 mph near Raskelf, north of York, on the Sunday 14.00 Kings Cross—Newcastle. 1st May, 1977.

J S Whiteley

Plate 28 Left   The tide appears to be well in as No 55 016 crosses the River Tweed on the Royal Border Bridge at Berwick heading a down express on 28th May, 1978.   *J S Whiteley*

Plate 29 Below   Miners' cottages are dwarfed by the slag heaps at Pegswood as the 08.00 Edinburgh—Kings Cross passes on 6th August, 1977.   *G W Morrison*

Plate 30 Above   On Easter Saturday 25th March, 1978 the up "Flying Scotsman" is passing Heaton.
P J Robinson

Plate 31 Below   No 55 017 is leaving Doncaster on 22nd June, 1977 on the up "Hull Pullman" which left Hull at 06.50 and reached Kings Cross at 09.55.
G W Morrison

Plate 32 Above   Speeding south on the up "Aberdonian" near Ouston Junction, Chester-le-Street, on 5th May, 1979.

R Lumley

Plate 33 Below   The down "Talisman" approaches Doncaster on 25th May, 1977 on its scheduled 5 hour 43 minute run to Edinburgh with stops at York, Darlington, Newcastle and Berwick.   *J S Whiteley*

55 019

Plate 34 Above On 4th April, 1977 No 55 019 snakes out of Doncaster at the head of the 12.40 Edinburgh–Kings Cross.
G W Morrison

Plate 35 Below At rest at its home depot of Haymarket on Monday 5th June, 1978. *G W Morrison*

Plate 36 Left On 4th June, 1977 No 55 020 rounds the curve off the Harrogate line as it approaches the ex Midland line at Wortley Junction, Leeds, heading the empty stock off the 11.25 Kings Cross—Harrogate back to Neville Hill carriage sidings.

G W Morrison

Plate 37 Below It is climbing out of Bradford on 18th May, 1977 with the 11.55 Bradford—Kings Cross. The entrance to Hammerton Street DMU depot is on the left in front of the signal box.

J S Whiteley

ARGYLL & SUTHERLAND HIGHLANDER

Plate 38 Above   No 55 021 stands at
Hull on the 12.45 to Kings Cross on
12th July, 1979.

G W Morrison

Plate 39 Right   It is passing the site of
Beeston station on 24th May, 1977 whilst
heading the 16.52 Harrogate—Kings
Cross.

G W Morrison

Plate 40 Below   The 09.20 Newcastle—
Kings Cross arriving at York on
3rd September, 1977.

J S Whiteley

Plate 41 Above   In two-tone green, No D 9000 passes Beeston, Leeds, on 29th June, 1965 heading a Leeds—Kings Cross express. It was renumbered 55 022 week ending 10th April, 1974.

G W Morrison

Plate 42 Left   On 6th June, 1979 it is climbing to Stoke Summit from Grantham on the 14.11 York—Kings Cross slow.

J S Whiteley

Plate 43 Below   A class 03 shunter is in evidence at Bradford Exchange whilst No 55 022 prepares to depart on the 17.30 to Kings Cross on 23rd March, 1979.

G W Morrison

late 44 Above   An unusual setting for No 55 017 *The Durham Light Infantry* on 23rd July, 1979. It is seen in the heart of
e Pennines at Black Rock, with Stalybridge Power Station in the background, whilst returning from Liverpool on the 17.05
York and Newcastle.   *L A Nixon*

Plate 45 Left
No 55 009 *Alycidon* is
leaving with the
Sunday 10.00 to
Aberdeen on 26th
September, 1976.
G W Morriso

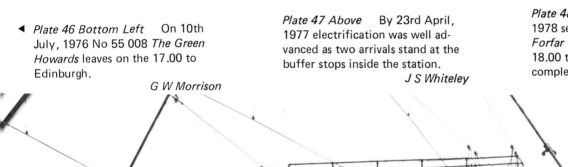

Plate 46 Bottom Left   On 10th July, 1976 No 55 008 *The Green Howards* leaves on the 17.00 to Edinburgh.

G W Morrison

Plate 47 Above   By 23rd April, 1977 electrification was well advanced as two arrivals stand at the buffer stops inside the station.

J S Whiteley

Plate 48 Below   11th September 1978 sees No 55 006 *The Fife & Forfar Yeomanry* leaving on the 18.00 to Edinburgh underneath the completed overhead electrification.

B Morrison

DELTIC PROFILES

Plate 49 Left   No D 9019 is seen in original two-tone green livery at Leeds Central on 6th March, 1962, just over two months after delivery. Note the horns mounted on the cab roof.

G W Morrison

Plate 50 Centre   No 55 009 *Alycidon* is at Holbeck shed on 13th September, 1977 in blue livery and looking decidedly the worse for wear.

G W Morrison

Plate 51 Bottom   On 30th July, 1977 No 55 003 *Meld* is on shed at Finsbury Park and has had the route indicator panel filled in. The "Flying Scotsman" thistle headboard was added for decorative purposes only!

G W Morrison

ATTENTION IN WORKS AND ON SHED

Plate 52 Right   On 19th August, 1979
No 55 022 *Royal Scots Grey* receives
attention inside Doncaster Works. On
the right can be seen No 50 025
Invincible.

B Morrison

Plate 53 Below   No 55 012 *Crepello*
receives attention to its paintwork
inside Finsbury Park on Saturday,
6th May, 1978 before working the first
"Hull Executive" on the following
Monday.

G W Morrison

Plate 54 Above   On 4th August, 1979 No 55 009 *Alycidon* emerges from
Calton Tunnel on arrival at Edinburgh Waverley with the 13.20 from Newcastle,
effectively the 16.05 from Dunbar. During the closure of Penmanshiel Tunnel in
1979 from 17th March until 20th August, East Coast passenger services were re-
vised involving some diversions from Newcastle to Carlisle, certain trains
being re-routed via the West Coast main line and the remainder of trains from the
South terminating at Berwick. A bus link was introduced between Berwick and
Dunbar with a connecting train service to Edinburgh and beyond.

G W Morrison

TUNNEL EXITS

Plate 55 Below   No 55 022 *Royal Scots Grey* bursts
out of Peascliffe Tunnel, just north of Grantham, on
the 08.00 Kings Cross—Edinburgh. 27th May, 1978.

G W Morrison

Plate 56 Right The 11.55 Bradford—Kings Cross is accelerated out of Ardsley Tunnel, between Leeds and Wakefield, by No 55 010 *The King's Own Scottish Borderer* on 18th May, 1977.

J S Whiteley

Plate 57 Below No 55 022 *Royal Scots Grey* eases into Kings Cross as it emerges from Gas Works Tunnel on 11th September, 1978 heading the 14.13 from York.

B Morrison

YORK IN DIFFERENT GUISES

Plate 58 Left   The Sunday 10.00 Kings Cross—Aberdeen is leaving Platform 9 on 16th January, 1977 behind No 55 006 *The Fife & Forfar Yeomanry*.

J S Whiteley

Plate 59 Bottom   Very few people are about as No 55 008 *The Green Howards* stops on the 20.00 Kings Cross—Aberdeen sleeper. 2nd October, 1979.

J S Whiteley

Plate 60 Above   Motive power past and present at York on Sunday 19th March, 1978 during BBC filming. No 55 013 *The Black Watch* is flanked by Gresley streamlined Pacific *Mallard* and an HST unit.

G W Morrison

Plate 61 Below   Will *The Black Watch* last as long as Stirling's Single of 1870?

G W Morrison

THE SILVER JUBILEE

Plate 62 Above The "Silver Jubilee" ra[n] during the summer of 1977 to commemo rate the Silver Jubilee of Queen Elizabeth II. Special headboards were cast and the train left Kings Cross at 07.45 arriving at Edinburgh at 13.20. The up train left Waverley station at 15.00 and arrived at Kings Cross at 20.37 and is seen on 15th July, 1977 passing through Manors Station, Newcastle, behind No 55 022 *Royal Scots Grey*.

P J Robinso[n]

Plate 63 Left The honour of hauling the "Silver Jubilee" was given to the Deltics, although on occasions class 47s deputised. No 55 021 *Argyll & Sutherlan[d] Highlander* passes Bridge Junction, Doncaster, on the down train whilst No 40 085 passes with an up grain train. 22nd June, 1977.

G W Morriso[n]

Plate 64 Right   The up train races through the junctions at Benton Quarry, north of Newcastle, behind No 55 004 *Queen's Own Highlander* on 19th July, 1977.

P J Robinson

Plate 65 Below   No 55 015 *Tulyar* is caught by a brief ray of sun on the climb to the summit at Grantshouse heading the down train on 17th August, 1977.

J S Whiteley

Plate 66 Above Spanning the River Tweed at Berwick-upon-Tweed is the magnificent Royal Border Bridge, which in pre-grouping days connected the North Eastern Railway with the North British Railway. No 55 022 *Royal Scots Grey* crosses at low tide on 17th August, 1977 heading the up "Flying Scotsman".

G W Morrison

Plate 67 Left Chester-le-Street viaduct sees No 55 00? *The Prince of Wales's Own Regiment of Yorkshire* crossing with the last up "Tees—Tyne Pullman" on 31st March 1976.

J R P Hunt

Plate 68 Above   Very wintry conditions in the North East on 11th January, 1977 sees No 55 014 *The Duke of Wellington's Regiment* crossing Plawsworth viaduct on an up express.
J R P Hunt

Plate 69 Below   In the very early morning of 8th July, 1979, No 55 007 *Pinza* crosses Yarm viaduct, spanning the River Tees, with the Sunday 00.05 Kings Cross—Newcastle sleeper, diverted via Stockton because of engineering work on the main line. The rather unstable state of the viaduct can clearly be seen in this picture.
R Lumley

Plate 70 Above   During the Autumn of 1961 the main line between Leeds and Wakefield was closed on Sundays because of engineering work, and trains were diverted via Low Moor and Spen Valley to Horbury and Wakefield. No D 9009 *Alycidon* passes Cleckheaton on 8th October, 1961 on the diverted 10.10 Leeds—Kings Cross.

J S Whiteley

Plate 71 Below   On Monday 23rd July, 1979 No 55 017 *The Durham Light Infantry* was unexpectedly diagrammed on a York—Liverpool train. It is seen returning on the 17.05 Liverpool—Newcastle as it passes Morley.

G W Morrison

Plate 72 Above   On Sunday 17th June, 1979 the 08.40 Kings Cross—Newcastle was diverted between Doncaster and York because of engineering work, and it is seen passing Knottingley behind No 55 021 *Argyll & Sutherland Highlander.*
N Stead

Plate 73 Below   The dereliction of Normanton, once such an important station. No 55 018 *Ballymoss* is passing on the Sunday 08.30 Hull—Kings Cross on 8th July 1979, diverted because of engineering work just north of Doncaster.
G W Morrison

Plate 74 Above   No 55 019 *Royal Highland Fusilier*
outside the refuelling depot at Gateshead on
13th June, 1979.   *R Lumley*

Plate 75 Below   Finsbury Park on 31st July, 1977 sees
Nos 55 013 *The Black Watch* and 55 003 *Meld*.
                                    G W Morrison

Plate 76 Above   Very unusual partners at Tinsley on Saturday 21st April, 1979. No 55 022 *Royal Scots Grey* is coming off shed to work a special train organised by the North Eastern Locomotive Preservation Group back to Newcastle (see also Plate 44). Earlier in the day it had brought the train from Middlesbrough to York and run light engine to Tinsley whilst the preserved *Green Arrow* brought the special South from York.

G W Morrison

Plate 77 Right   No D 9004, as yet un-named and barely 2 months old, is seen inside Haymarket on 17th July, 1961.

J S Whiteley

BETWEEN EDINBURGH AND BERWICK

Plate 78 Top   Soon after leaving Edinburgh, No 55 011 *The Royal Northumberland Fusiliers* nears Monktonhall Junction with the 17.50 to Leeds on Sunday 4th June 1978.

G W Morrison

Plate 79 Left   On 17th July, 196 No D 9006, unnamed and only about three weeks old, leaves Dunbar on the 07.30 Aberdeen— Kings Cross.

J S Whitele

Plate 80 Below   No 55 013 *The Black Watch* passes the summit at Grantshouse with the Saturdays only 07.55 Kings Cross—Edinburgh on 6th August, 1977.

G W Morriso

Plate 81 Above   On 3rd June, 1978 No 55 018 *Ballymoss* is seen on the 17.10 Edinburgh—Berwick-upon-Tweed local near Millerhill.

G W Morrison

Plate 82 Below   No 55 007 *Pinza* drifts downhill from Grantshouse with the up "Aberdonian", the 10.35 Aberdeen—Kings Cross, on Saturday 6th August, 1977.

G W Morrison

ON THE HARROGATE LINE

Plate 83 Above   On 25th May, 1963 No D9021, as yet unnamed, passes Wortley Junction on the down "Queen of Scots Pullman", the train having reversed at Leeds Central.

J S Whiteley

Plate 84 Below   A very different scene at Wortley Junction, Leeds, or 17th September, 1977 when No 55 015 *Tulyar* takes the Harrogate line on the Saturday 11.25 Kings Cross—Harrogate. The picture above was taken from the signal box which used to stand above the cab of No 55 (in this picture. The former GN line seen in the background of the above picture, together with Leeds Central station, have now sadly disappeare from the modern scene.

J S White

Plate 85 Above   On Good Friday
13th April, 1979 No 55 003 *Meld*
approaches Wescoe Hill Tunnel near
Weeton with the 09.04 Harrogate—
Kings Cross. At this date *Meld* had
only just been given its white cab
roofs and this was one of its first
workings in this condition.
                    J S Whiteley

Plate 86 Right   One of the main
features of the Harrogate line is
Bramhope Tunnel, 2 miles 241 yards
in length. On 12th February, 1977
No 55 010 *The King's Own Scottish
Borderer* is approaching the tunnel
on the 11.25 Kings Cross—Harrogate.
                    G W Morrison

LEEDS TO BRADFORD

Plate 87 Left The long and short of it at Bradford Exchange on Sunday 8th July, 1979. No 55 010 *The King's Own Scottish Borderer* is waiting to leave on the 16.15 to Kings Cross whilst No 03 047 is in the parcels bay.

G W Morrison

Plate 88 Below A powerful picture of No 55 013 *The Black Watch* storming out of Hammerton Street Tunnel with the 17.30 Bradford—Kings Cross on 2nd May, 1979.

G W Morrison

Plate 89 Above No 55 005 *The Prince of Wales's Own Regiment of Yorkshire* is climbing towards Laisterdyke on the 12.45 Kings Cross—Bradford on 23rd April, 1979.
J S Whiteley

Plate 90 Right The site of the now demolished station at Laisterdyke can be seen behind the rear of the train in this picture of No 55 015 *Tulyar* heading the 12.45 Kings Cross—Bradford on 9th May, 1979, less than one week before HST units took over West Riding Inter-City services. The line in the foreground is freight only to Bowling Junction.
J S Whiteley

BETWEEN DURHAM
AND BERWICK-UPON-TWEED

Plate 91 Above No 55 012 *Crepello* is leaving Heaton carriage sidings, Newcastle, on 25th June, 1979 with the stock of the 20.30 Newcastle—Kings Cross.

R Lumley

Plate 92 Below On 8th June, 1977 No 55 012 *Crepello* is passing Alnmouth with the inaugural down "Silver Jubilee".

J S Whiteley

Plate 93 Above   A bird's eye view of the northern approach to Newcastle taken from the Castle Keep, with Manors station just visible at the rear of the train. No 55 003 *Meld* is observing the 15 mph speed restriction heading the up "Flying Scotsman" on Saturday 14th May, 1977.

G W Morrison

Plate 94 Above   Market day at Chester-le-Street on 12th May, 1978. An unidentified Deltic passes almost un-noticed in the background, high up on the viaduct, heading an up morning express to Kings Cross.

J R P Hunt

Plate 95 Below   A glimpse of Durham viaduct between the terraced houses sees No 55 014 *The Duke of Wellington's Regiment* crossing with the 08.50 Edinburgh—Plymouth in May 1979. At this period, during the closure of Penmanshiel Tunnel, Deltics were diagrammed to work this train from Berwick-upon-Tweed to York, working to Berwick on the 08.10 from Newcastle.

J R P Hunt

Plate 96 Above   A rather more traditional view of the
magnificent Durham viaduct sees No 55 014 *The Duke of
Wellington's Regiment* crossing on 12th May, 1979 heading
the Saturday 15.00 Kings Cross—Edinburgh and
Aberdeen, diverted via Carlisle from Newcastle due to the
collapse of Penmanshiel Tunnel.

N Stead

Plate 97 Below   No 55 005 *The Prince of Wales's Own
Regiment of Yorkshire* speeds northwards near Durham
with the 14.00 Kings Cross—Aberdeen on 15th August,
1976.

P J Robinson

AT LINCOLN

Plate 98 Left   On Sunday 22nd October 1978 the 09.15 Bradford–Kings Cross approaches Lincoln Central behind No 55 008 *The Green Howards*. The train had been diverted because of engineering works affecting Peascliffe Tunnel.

J Marsh

Plate 99 Below   Lincoln Cathedral dominates this picture taken on Saturday 12th May, 1979. No 55 009 *Alycidon* is leaving Lincoln St Marks on the 17.33 Cleethorpes–Kings Cross.

G W Morrison

Plate 100 Above   No 55 009 *Alycidon* shortly after passing Lincoln St Marks with the 13.04 Kings Cross—Cleethorpes on Saturday 12th May, 1979.

G W Morrison

Plate 101 Below   After a brief stop at Lincoln St Marks, the 13.05 Kings Cross—Cleethorpes is accelerated away by No 55 021 *Argyll & Sutherland Highlander*, due to arrive at Cleethorpes at 16.28. 28th July, 1979.

G W Morrison

CLEETHORPES TRAINS

Plate 102 Above   A pleasing blend of old and new at Roxton Sidings near Habrough in this picture of the 13.05 Kings Cross—Cleethorpes taken on 13th September, 1979. No 55 007 *Pinza* is dominated by the GN somersault signal and attractive signal box, memories of a bygone age.   *L A Nixon*

Plate 103 Left   No 55 021 *Argyll & Sutherland Highlander* nears its journey's end between Grimsby Town and Cleethorpes on the 13.05 from Kings Cross. 28th July, 1979.   *G W Morrison*

Plate 104 Below   With the North Sea just visible in the background and an amusement park adjacent to the station, No 55 021 *Argyll & Sutherland Highlander* shunts the empty stock off the Kings Cross train on 28th July, 1979.   *G W Morrison*

NORTH HUMBERSIDE

Plate 105 Right   The Humber Bridge can be seen in the background of this picture showing No 55 017 *The Durham Light Infantry* passing Ferriby with the 12.45 Hull–Kings Cross.

G W Morrison

Plate 106 Below   The magnificent overall roof of the ex North Eastern Railway terminus of Paragon station still exists, as can be seen in this picture of No 55 021 *Argyll & Sutherland Highlander* leaving Hull on the 12.45 to Kings Cross on 12th July, 1979.

G W Morrison

Plate 107 Top On 14th May, 1963 No D 9019, still unnamed, speeds past Doncaster North on a Newcastle—Kings Cross train.

J S Whiteley

Plate 108 Right With a steam standby in evidence at the south end of the station, No D 9017 passes non-stop on the up "Tees-Tyne Pullman".

J S Whiteley

Plate 109 Below The up "Talisman" speeds through the station on the centre road on 14th May, 1963 behind No D 9021.

J S Whiteley

Plate 110 Bottom By 14th May, 1963 No D 9001 had been given the name *St Paddy*, and it is seen after arrival at Doncaster on a trial run from Kings Cross with a dynamometer car attached to the engine. Note also the position of the BR emblems.

J S Whiteley

FOCUS ON DONCASTER

Plate 111 Above　　The multi-storey car park gives a good view of the north end of Doncaster, and on 7th July, 1977 No 55 017 *The Durham Light Infantry* is slowing for its stop on the 08.30 Newcastle—Kings Cross.

G W Morrison

Plate 112 Below　　The full extent of the "Plant" can also be seen from the multi-storey car park, and on 19th June, 1978 No 55 014 *The Duke of Wellington's Regiment* is leaving with the 08.00 Kings Cross—Edinburgh.

G W Morrison

Plate 113 Above   About two miles south of Doncaster, the Lincoln line diverges from the East Coast main line at Black Carr Junction. On 11th September, 1977 No 55 001 *St Paddy* takes the Lincoln line with the Sunday 10.30 Newcastle—Kings Cross, diverted via Lincoln because of engineering work on the main line. At this period the junction was being remodelled, the Lincoln connection was being singled and the semaphore signals, for so long a feature of the junction, had just been replaced with colour lights.

J S Whiteley

BLACK CARR JUNCTION

Plate 114 Below   Earlier in 1977, on 12th March, the semaphore signals were still in use and No 55 003 *Meld* accelerates the 10.50 Newcastle—Kings Cross up the main line.

P J Robinson

SOUTH OF DONCASTER

Plate 115 Above   On 23rd September, 1962, still in original
two-tone green livery without yellow warning panels,
No D 9008 is climbing to Askham Tunnel south of Retford
with an Edinburgh—Kings Cross.

T Boustead

Plate 116 Top Right   Framed by the then A1 road bridge,
No D 9006 passes Grantham with the up "Flying Scotsman"
on 20th July, 1963.

T Boustead

Plate 117 Right   No D 9007 *Pinza* is seen on 12th September,
1964, just south of Newark, heading the up "Flying Scotsman"
during the period when the thistle headboard was in use on the
train.

T Boustead

Plate 118 Below   On Saturday 30th July, 1977 No 55 002
The King's Own Yorkshire Light Infantry roars up Holloway
Bank with the 18.00 to Newcastle.

G W Morrison

ALONGSIDE THE SEA

Plate 119 Above   One of the most picturesque stretches of the East Coast main line is just north of Berwick-upon-Tweed, and on 7th June, 1977 No 55 020 *Nimbus* is near Burnmouth heading the 08.00 Kings Cross—Edinburgh.

J S Whiteley

Plate 120 Below   No 55 022 *Royal Scots Grey* hurries a Kings Cross—Edinburgh express along the cliff tops at Lamberton Beach near Berwick-upon-Tweed on 16th July, 1977.

L A Nixon

Plate 121 Above   The estuary of the River Tweed can be seen in this picture taken near Spittal, just south of Berwick-upon-Tweed, on the fine clear day of 9th May, 1979. No 55 007 *Pinza* is heading an up afternoon express to Kings Cross.   *N Stead*

Plate 122 Right   On Saturday 10th March, 1979, just before the collapse of Penmanshiel Tunnel, the up "Aberdonian" passes the Border sign at Marshal Meadows behind No 55 019 *Royal Highland Fusilier.*

N Stead

Plate 123 Below   A fine view of No 55 017 *The Durham Light Infantry* on the 17.00 Edinburgh—Kings Cross running along the cliff tops near Burnmouth on 2nd June, 1978.

G W Morrison

NOCTURNE

Plate 124 Above   Platform 16 at York sees No 55 006 *The Fife & Forfar Yeomanry* at about 21.00 after arrival on the 18.05 stopper from Kings Cross. 2nd October, 1979.

J S Whiteley

Plate 125 Below   Shortly before departure from Kings Cross, No 55 001 *St Paddy* is seen on the "Night Aberdonian", the 22.15 sleeper to Aberdeen.

B Morrison

SELBY

Plate 126 Right   An unidentified Deltic crosses the River Ouse on the famous swing bridge with a down express in March 1964. Selby North signal box and the station can be seen in the background.

J S Whiteley

Plate 127 Below   On 10th September, 1977 the up "Aberdonian" makes its Saturdays only stop at Selby behind No 55 021 *Argyll & Sutherland Highlander.* The signal box straddling the swing bridge from which the adjoining photograph was taken can be seen above the rear of the train.

L A Nixon

TRANS PENNINE

Plate 128 Left   Occasionally during 1979 Deltics have been diagrammed on Liverpool trains from either Newcastle or York. Saturday 8th September, 1979 was one such day when No 55 018 *Ballymoss* visited Merseyside. It is seen nearing Batley whilst returning on the 16.05 Liverpool—Newcastle.

G W Morrison

Plate 129 Below   Earlier in the day it had worked to Liverpool on the 09.28 from Newcastle, and is seen climbing through Paddock cutting shortly after leaving Huddersfield.

G W Morrison

Plate 130 Above   During the closure of Penmanshiel Tunnel in 1979 from 17th March until 20th August, certain trains were diverted from Newcastle via Carlisle to Edinburgh. One such train was the 05.50 Kings Cross—Edinburgh and it is seen on 15th August passing Hexham behind No 55 015 *Tulyar*.

R Lumley

PENMANSHIEL DIVERSIONS

Plate 131 Below   The same train is seen on Saturday 4th August, 1979 climbing Beattock Bank behind No 55 003 *Meld.* An electric-hauled up Inter-City train is passing on its way south from Glasgow.

G W Morrison

BALLYMOSS VISITS LIVERPOOL

Plate 132 Left   At about 13.10 on Saturday 8th September, 1979, trainspotters on the platform end at Liverpool Lime Street got a surprise when No 55 018 *Ballymoss* emerged from Lime Street cutting with the 09.28 from Newcastle.

Plate 133 Right   Pursued by spotters, it is backing out of the platform after removal of the stock.

Plate 134 Below   It returned across the Pennines on the 16.05 to Newcastle and is seen standing on its train surrounded by onlookers, with the station clock showing 15.22.
All G W Morrison

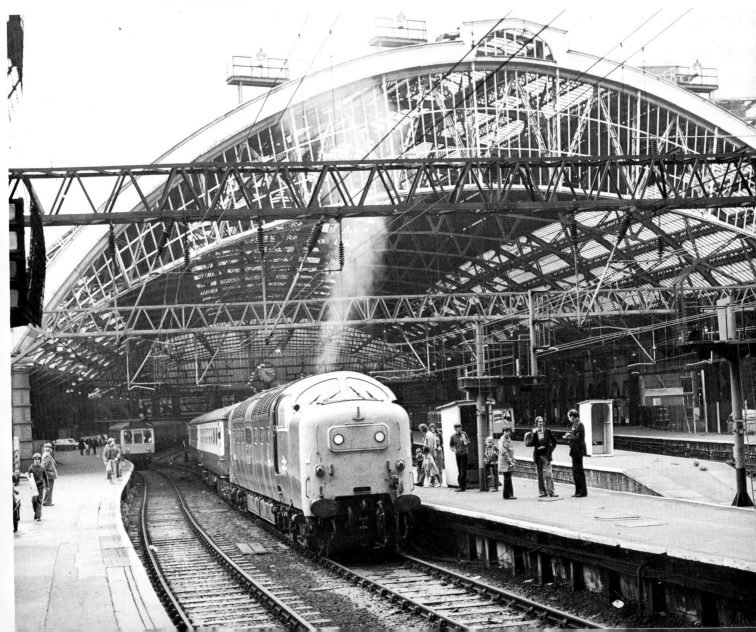

IN THE NORTH EAST

Plate 135 Above   No 55 010 *The King's Own Scottish Borderer* passes Darlington MPD as it approaches Bank Top station with the 10.20 Newcastle—Kings Cross on 21st April, 1979.

R Lumley

Plate 136 Below   A relief Edinburgh—Kings Cross is seen passing Sunderland Bridge near Durham on 30th May, 1978 behind No 55 002 *The King's Own Yorkshire Light Infantry.*

G W Morrison

Plate 137 Right   Due to the collapse of
an embankment near Durham on Sunday
1st April, 1979, No 55 019 *Royal Highland
Fusilier* takes the coast route with the
retimed 13.10 Edinburgh—Kings Cross. It
is seen crossing the Monkwearmouth
Bridge as it approaches Sunderland.
N Stead

Plate 138 Below   It is seen again, further
on its journey south, passing through
Stockton, just before removal of the
overall station roof.   *N Stead*

AROUND GRANTHAM

Plate 139 Left No D9019 nears Grantham after its descent from Stoke Summit heading an afternoon Kings Cross—Edinburgh express on 12th April, 1963.

T Boustead

Plate 140 Below About two miles north of Grantham is Peascliffe Tunnel, and on 6th June, 1979 No 55 010 *The King's Own Scottish Borderer* emerges into glorious sunshine heading the 15.50 York—Kings Cross.

J S Whiteley

Plate 141 Above   On 14th July, 1979 No 55 011 *The Royal Northumberland Fusiliers* accelerates the 14.05 Kings Cross—York away from its brief stop at Grantham and approaches Peascliffe Tunnel. The spire of Grantham Church can be seen on the horizon.

G W Morrison

Plate 142 Below   No 55 011 *The Royal Northumberland Fusiliers* is seen again as it passes Grantham station non-stop with an up express on 17th October, 1976.   *J S Whiteley*

Plate 143 Left On Sunday 10th July, 1977 No 55 007 *Pin* approaches Rotherham station Masboro Station South Junctio on a BR special from Chesterfie to Carlisle, having just picked u passengers at Sheffield.

G W Mor

Plate 144 Below On what is normally a freight only line, No 55 022 *Royal Scots Grey* passes Tinsley marshalling yard heading a return special to Newcastle (see also Plate 76). It just taken over from two class 7 electrics which had brought the train from the Dinting Railway Centre via the Woodhead route. 21st April, 1979. *J S Whit*

Plate 145 Right Soon after leaving Sheffield, No 55 003 *Meld* passes Brightside on 23rd July, 1978 heading a BR special excursion from Chesterfield to Carlisle and Newcastle.
G W Morrison

Plate 146 Below On Sunday 8th July, 1979 No 55 018 *Ballymoss* is seen on the 08.30 Hull—Kings Cross passing underneath the Tinsley Viaduct which carries the M1 motorway on the upper level. It had been diverted via Selby, Burton Salmon, Normanton, Aldwarke Junction, Darnall and Worksop, returning to the East Coast main line at Retford. *L A Nixon*

LEEDS— CARLISLE

Plate 147 Left The picturesque Eden Valley near Armathwaite sees No 55 012 *Crepello* on 20th May, 1978 heading the "Thames—Forth Express", a special from St. Pancras to Edinburgh organised by the Lea Valley Railway Club.　　*P J Robinso*

Plate 148 Below On 17th June, 1967 one of the faste ever journeys from Carlisle Skipton via the Settle and Carlisle line over Ais Gill was recorded. No D9005 *The Prince of Wales's Own Regiment of Yorkshire* covered the 86.8 miles in 72 minutes 47 seconds on t return "Hadrian Flyer", and it is seen further on its journey passing Holbeck Low Level as it approaches Leeds.　　*J Mar*

Plate 149 Above   The Midland signal gantries at Guiseley Junction, Shipley, dominate this picture of No 55 009 *Alycidon* on a special organised by the Deltic Preservation Society from York to Carnforth on the murky morning of Sunday 14th October, 1979.   *J S Whiteley*

Plate 150 Below   No 55 016 *Gordon Highlander* leaves Skipton on 27th October, 1979 heading a special organised by the LCGB from Liverpool to Carlisle and Glasgow via Leeds and the Settle and Carlisle line.

                                                                    G W Morrison

NOT FOR THE ENVIRONMENTALISTS!

Plate 151 Left   No 55 021 *Argyll & Sutherland Highlander* erupts from beneath an overbridge Bensham, shortly after coming off the King Edward Bridge, making a typical "cold start" with the 09.20 Newcastle–Kings Cross on 28th May, 1977.   *P J Robinson*

Plate 152 Below   On 24th April, 1979 No 55 018 *Ballymoss* covers Bradford with a cloud of light blue exhaust, peculiar to Deltics, as it starts the 17.30 to Kings Cross on only one engine.   *J S Whiteley*